promiscuous beauty

poems by

Martin Arnold

Finishing Line Press
Georgetown, Kentucky

promiscuous beauty

Copyright © 2019 by Martin Arnold
ISBN 978-1-64662-065-4 First Edition
All rights reserved under International and Pan-American Copyright Conventions. No part of this book may be reproduced in any manner whatsoever without written permission from the publisher, except in the case of brief quotations embodied in critical articles and reviews.

Publisher: Leah Maines

Editor: Christen Kincaid

Cover Art: Ann Arnold

Author Photo: Ann Arnold

Cover Design: Elizabeth Maines McCleavy

Printed in the USA on acid-free paper.
Order online: www.finishinglinepress.com
also available on amazon.com

Author inquiries and mail orders:
Finishing Line Press
P. O. Box 1626
Georgetown, Kentucky 40324
U. S. A.

Table of Contents

Caution Sign Riddled With Bullet Holes ... 1

Dream of the Voyage ... 2

General Electric ... 3

There Is No Poop Fairy ... 4

Implied Narratives ... 5

Promiscuous Beauty ... 6

Endless Variations on the Same Theme ... 7

Splitting Hairs ... 8

Youth ... 9

Promiscuous Beauty ... 10

Venus at the Pool ... 11

Being Wanted ... 12

Friends in High Places ... 13

Innocent Gestures ... 14

Promiscuous Beauty ... 16

Privilege ... 18

Journey Made Entirely of Waiting ... 20

Little Star ... 21

Caution Sign Riddled with Bullet Holes

Tread sunk in the sod where corner lot meets both streets.

There are two types of people in this world:
Those who cuss the ugliness of mud ruts
And those who cultivate impatiens in the careless driver's path.

Some of us pretend we can live without love
Because the heart's always in a hurry, rolling through stop signs,
Scanning the airwaves for a livelier station,

Oblivious to what it crushes
Beneath its incomprehensible weight.

Dream of the Voyage

Plywood and two-by-fours, a simple shelter
on an overturned table; buoyed

by my father's optimism, we raft to South America,
our cargo just a handful of books. It's summer.

We strike a fire, one infernal sail
casting shadow monsters, exchange stories bundled

in silence. No rudder, motor, or paddles. We drift above
schools of our former worries. We feed our hunger

starlight. The current is our captain
and he's in love with the moon.

General Electric

Pansy cogs and dogwood factories.
A pollution of pollen.

Insect static above field of untamed grass.

The last light coursing through the grid
Of crisscrossing web.

There Is No Poop Fairy

You couldn't pull a more gorgeous morning out of a hat:
The breeze is an incantation whispered
Over sage and yucca, tumbleweed and rose;

The clouds are drop biscuits dolloped on a glass tray;
And one bold quail serenades every female in the canyon.

It's summer, and I don't remember
What day of the week it is
Which doesn't seem to bother
The roadrunners and cottontails,
Butterflies, stinkbugs, and coyotes

Or even the millions of ants tunneling beneath this trail
With its new pink signs
Where a burly man in a tiara
In tights and lace wings
Shakes his wand at inconsiderate dog walkers.

Some days the laziness of others makes me smile
Just as sometimes foolishness is a blessing.

Like those fences blocking long views at state parks
Erected after someone leaning out for a selfie
Plunges to his death—

Because when they build the fence they also build a gift shop
With carousels of post card

More beautiful than we could ever take.

Implied Narratives

The gun shop shares a billboard with a carpet cleaner.

The new glass-walled high school
Stares down into the county landfill
Where the wind pins papers against the high fence.

Leagues of shade from cottonwoods along a river of sand.

At The Alibi, you can buy liquor while filling your tank.

A man's smile is distorted through the heat rising
From his wife's mocha chino.

When he calls, her phone sings,
"It's the end of the world as we know it."

A cashier pushes her spoon through a muffin
Like a passenger train plunging into a hillside.

When rain falls, the valley exhales
After holding its breath for months.

Over time, the tattoo of his mother weeps.

The only part of town where church bells still ring
Is the tourist district.

We've raised the stars above our streets
And can no longer see heaven in the constellations.

Promiscuous Beauty

Out here, days stretch between barbs, between the hum of tires
crossing cattle guards, in the lean of livestock chutes
near the graveyard of pickups. In clusters

of small homes: boxes with gray and green asphalt siding.
No observable occupations
beyond the slow rocking of a dozen scattered pump jacks

except for the husbandry of a few cattle
this stingy landscape sustains.

Two satellite dishes. One RV with char
around a melted hole that once housed a window.

There's too much junk in my life, the starkness suggests, obstacles
which keep me from becoming

a cartographer of clouds and confidant of stars, a recorder
of the movement of boulders, an acolyte of the wind
as it strips all surface vegetation

to reveal the stone truth

beneath it all.

Endless Variations on the Same Theme

A study in patience, in ocular grace, an apprenticeship
in awareness, to capture each minute shift

of the breeze across a maple leaf,
its architecture of veins, its tongue
curling to savor yesterday's rain,

the leaf's subtle and infinitely intriguing
variations due to temperature and humidity,
to climate, nutrition, and location,

to the particular critter habitat it composes
and dozens of other factors I haven't yet considered ...

each glittering uniqueness magnified
beyond a foundation of similarities.

We each have obsessions we endlessly explore,
unpacking the tiny and almost imperceptible shifts,
the barely discernable changes,

getting closer to understanding the true subject
isn't the leaf or the tree or the loosening boulder with
the abandoned corral in its path—

that the more we lose ourselves in that gaze

the clearer it becomes
the true subject

is always the same.

Splitting Hairs

Hair We Go or better yet
Curl Up and Dye.

Even someone with as little
need as I can admire this
clever cleaver
to the cliché, this hair splinter

to the predictable's
cuticle, the pedestrian scissors
guided by a bowl

or at least clippings unswept
from the shoulder sweat
ignites. Too often,

in conversation
I can't tell where hair shirt
ends and hirsute begins.

Why aren't there more riots up our spines?

More children hungover wobbling home
after all-day good-book benders?

We live in … you know what kind of situation I mean.

But in language thankfully there are
Strands of Hope and Locks of Luck.

There are Gods of Style.
So Weave Mystery. Tangled in Beauty.

Youth

We think youth's the sculpted abdomen
Of a marble torso
Time decapitates

But youth's really that head
Unable to imagine its body
Living on without it.

Promiscuous Beauty

For some reason today I'm thinking of beautiful Jessica
With her eyes that were deep wells of sorrow.

I'm thinking of how late we were to the dance that evening
We kissed in the parking garage:

Those coiling ringlets of darkness drilling into my cheeks,
The thumbs up of a passing chaperone,

The labyrinth of that elaborate dress, those impenetrable undergarments,
My frustration when she refused to go any farther,

The same foolishness that drove me from her cousin
I was in love with
After we made-out on a bench
In a park no streets touched.

Back then I never suspected
I wasn't capable of love

Just as I never thought after all these years
It would be the pleasure I'd remember,

How that pleasure seemed inexhaustible
Like the aquafers beneath us

Our eighth grade science teacher inaccurately claimed
Were too vast for humans to drain.

Venus at the Pool

The sacred dwells inside the pedestrian
Occasionally rising to the surface
In moments like this

In the shallows where the waves wash up the gradual slope
To tease the shore, to flirt with it

Before vanishing into the hidden drains
Where the tiles read 0 FEET and NO DIVING,

In this mother standing with her three daughters
In the scalloped waters.

The crowd parts. Whistling lifeguards, and the perfume of chlorine.

It isn't the way the breeze uncoils her blonde ringlets
Or her partially clad classical proportions
That draw all eyes her way;

It's that relaxed, natural confidence
In the slight tilt of the head
Under this veil of clouds
That makes the light fuzzy

As if the universe were recreating
The famous painting by Botticelli

While making a few updates:

Three graces;
The swimsuit's gesture of modesty;

The tattooed pistols
Tucked into the lacey fringes of her bikini—

Ivory-handled ovaries and barrels targeting
This breathtaking mystery.

Being Wanted

It's the neighbor drifting in her wheelchair
down the center of our street
with three dogs in orbit.

It's a line of cars, the hand's hesitation
hovering above horn, the leash

holding hand in check, the sound of those horns
unwired. It's the shadow

of a robin on the far wall
grown too large for its branch. It's

the branch bending beneath that growing.

It's the spider inching toward the beak
which cannot swallow it, the air
fluttering those featherless wings,

the stink from the pear blossom
seeping through the glass

where the robin passes through it.

It's the teen spreading out her flowered towel,
a bikini with a hint of coconut, the boys

on the track as they slow
around the bend near her yard.

It's the way the whole field tilts
beneath their longing.

Friends in High Places

Sparrows sing from the rafters of the home improvement warehouse
despite the performer on the radio

who blames his low upbringing
for ruining his ex's wedding

before sinking to the bottom of a bottle
where friends dwell. Such determination

in the birds as they push through his voice
until this singer is a gurgling brook, until this

country song is a tobacco barn
split by oaks and strangled by wisteria.

If they drift out the automatic doors today
they'll catch charred aspen on the breeze from Vallecito

and if they're vigilant they'll notice
the Harris Hawk's nest in the tallest cottonwood

but inside this strange cave these birds are free
to sing unapologetically,

even if their friends who live outdoors
hear in the music drifting from the skylights

what the coyote hears in the yapping of a poodle
perched on a cushion

with a glitter-coated collar and a rubber bone
pinned under its paw.

Innocent Gestures

It's difficult not to pass judgement
on the pregnant teenage McDonalds cashier
leaning against the faux brick façade
in this inconsiderate November breeze

as she cups her hand
where the tip of a cigarette
hovers above the mouth of a lighter.

Once you stumble into knowledge,
the path back to oblivion is steep—
you're only chance really
is to turn off the television

before Dr. Oz models tar-clogged lungs
next to deformed newborns.

Still, there's an elegance to her gesture
poisoned by our disdain, simplicity's embodiment:

Strike. Strike. Cuss.
Strike. Strike. Shake.

And who are we to be offended
by the cruel way nature lavishes gifts

on those we suspect
could never appreciate them
like we could?

And what do we know about her life
past the uniform and nametag?

Insulated in an SUV
worth more than she makes a year,

we head to the off-season beach home we've rented
with a deck reaching out over the tides

that never feel like a lecture
about giving up something
we've developed a taste for,

waves rolling in like an old friend
who tells us what we want to hear
over and over again.

Promiscuous Beauty

The sparseness of the desert willow leaves suggests
we don't have to hoard all the sunlight,

that we can take what we need and let the rest fall
to the goat heads and scrub brush and dandelions at our feet,

and the slenderness of the leaves suggests there's an elegance in modesty,
a pride in being humble,

which seems contradicted by the way the leaves cluster
in bursts of exploding fireworks

until you remember there are more varieties of trees
than there are personalities,

more seasons than there are weeks;
and this time of summer there's an overwhelming sense

the party's over, we're too late,
we missed some amazing blowout
recently

judging by the tinsel of dried seed pods
draping from the branches.

The multiple twisting trunks supporting the canopy
imply the power of community
as well as the need for it

and are not the symptoms of a split personality
to be hospitalized, medicated, or therapied

because even if the maples near it
bully the desert willow for its inadequacies—

it's short and a little confused looking,
a poor shade provider,

not much of a bird sanctuary or a threat to kites—

this tree doesn't apologize for what it isn't,
this creature with its gorgeous orchestra of flowers,

those pink tunneling horns
which warp the air with music,

the distortion of vibrating wings
from everyone's favorite territorial sugar fiend.

Privilege

Some mornings it washes over me
With the massage of a thousand undocumented fingers,
Its heat erasing this visage from the mirror,

And the drain becomes a huddle of open mouths
From children who have traveled a long distance
Because their wells have dried up

Due in part to my tendency to daydream in the shower

And in part to what my car pumps into the atmosphere
On my commute each day
As I sip a steaming beverage of crushed beans
This part of the globe can't grow.

It isn't flattering to admit but most days
I drift as oblivious as a cloud
Over parched farmland
Before raining into the ocean,

And that part of me that insists I only shower
To ensure coworkers don't move away at lunch
Before discretely exchanging a calendar
For baking casseroles
Seasoned with extra pity

Is likely just another self-delusion.

If Privilege is a closed system
Where a few get more because the many get less,

Then the blood flooding my plate last night
Didn't flow from that New York strip

I gnawed until my tummy ached
Depositing an extra layer of fat
Around the abdomen
Like an insurance policy against an empty cupboard

Which makes sense if you think of privilege as an insulation
Which allows my family to crack open crustaceans
Dredged from the ocean's depths
Sitting at this table in the desert

Without imagining all the people in this small town
Hunger catches in its net.

And it's probably the result of privilege
That I stand here now thinking it would be nice
If the solution were as simple
As turning off the faucet
Four days a week

To lift the water in wells
Where villagers have set up internet cams

So I can witness the water table rising on my good deeds
As joyous children fill their earthen jugs,

So I can be sure I'm doing the right thing,
That my sacrifice has meaning,

And that I'm being appreciated for it.

Journey Made Entirely of Waiting

There's a place at Silence's center
the size of a grain of pollen
slipping from the leaf
as the wasp leaps from the dandelion.

Everything fits inside it—each serenade, bird song,
manifesto, car alarm, physics lecture, Big Bang.

It's a mountain you climb standing still,

a hundred mile gorge across the Ford to your father,
and mother's *If you don't have something nice to say ...*

It's an oak severing a power line, extinguishing
the television and the faithful buzzing of the lights,

each battery beautifully uncharged,
just quiet insulated in stillness

fragile as a bell before the hammer's strike.

Little Star

Nature in its infinitely intriguing variations, its genius
genetic stumblings, those lucky accidents, its dead ends
and limitless losses, its harmony of mutations:

The generation of light
to attract the meager nutritional morsel.

Because resources are scarce, anglerfish are forced to extreme measures
in relationships … the male attaches to the female

then shrinks to conserve food
like a considerate parasite
whose single purpose is to stay out of the way
as he waits around to fertilize the eggs.

Once I discovered a roommate cowering in the bathtub
as his girlfriend hammered her foot through the faux wood door;

even across the room I could see trouble reflected
in the steel blade she brandished.

Over time, the male anglerfish discards relics from his former life:

shot glass collection, photos of former friends, that carving of the nude
from Hawaii,
his fins, his mouth, his eyes. Maybe

for each of us there's a different boundary
between adoration and immolation.

I still see selfies of them on Facebook. They look happy.

So much of who we are is determined
between the semen and the egg,

and the vast majority of genetic deviations
reduce chances for survival.

All around us darkness then a little star.
We swim toward it. We can't help ourselves.

It's the most beautiful thing we've ever seen.

Martin Arnold has taught at numerous colleges and universities, including Guilford College, where he served as a Visiting Assistant Professor. He earned an MA from New Mexico State University and an MFA from the University of North Carolina at Greensboro. He has served as the poetry editor of The Greensboro Review, and as an assistant poetry editor for *storysouth* and *Puerto del Sol*. His work has been published in many fine journals including *Crazyhorse, the Carolina Review, Denver Quarterly,* and *Best New Poets 2012*. His first chapbook, *A Million Distant Glittering Catastrophes*, won the 2009-2010 Pavement Saw Chapbook Award. *Earthquake Owner's Manual* won the 2013 Unicorn Press First Book Award. He currently teaches at V. Sue Cleveland High School in Rio Rancho, New Mexico.

www.ingramcontent.com/pod-product-compliance
Lightning Source LLC
LaVergne TN
LVHW041525070426
835507LV00013B/1821